The Joy of Piano Duets

For centuries duet playing has held and continues to hold
a fascinating attraction for the student, the teacher, and the
professional musician. One of the most pleasurable
aspects of music-making, it always provides an enjoyable
experience to both player and audience. In addition, it has
definite pedagogical benefits.

The Joy Of Piano Duets contains colorful examples of
music from the classics to folk songs to jazz.
The arrangements are equally easy for both players with
the melody alternating between the two.

Robert Schumann advised pianists, "Don't omit any
opportunity to play with others." It is sound advise.
We trust that this collection will be a source of pleasure to
"one piano-four hands" enthusiasts the world over.

Order No. YK 21111
US International Standard Book Number: 0.8256.8008.5

Exclusive Distributors:
Music Sales Corporation
257 Park Avenue South, New York, NY 10010 USA
Music Sales Limited
8/9 Frith Street, London W1V 5TZ England
Music Sales Pty. Limited
120 Rothschild Street, Rosebery, Sydney, NSW 2018, Australia

Printed in the United States of America by
Vicks Lithograph and Printing Corporation

Contents

Bourrée
from Violin Sonata No. 2

Secondo

Johann Sebastian Bach

Bourrée
from Violin Sonata No. 2

Primo

Johann Sebastian Bach

The Trout

Franz Schubert

Moderately Secondo

The Trout

Primo

Franz Schubert

"The Metronome"
Theme from Symphony No. 8

Secondo

Ludwig van Beethoven

Lively, mechanical motion

"The Metronome"
Theme from Symphony No. 8

Primo

Lively, mechanical motion

Ludwig van Beethoven

Arioso

Secondo

Johann Sebastian Bach

Moderately slow

Arioso

Primo

Johann Sebastian Bach

Moderately slow

Rondino
Theme from Cello Concerto in D

Secondo

Joseph Haydn

Rondino
Theme from Cello Concerto in D

Primo

Joseph Haydn

D. C. al Fine

Caprice No. 24

Secondo

Niccolo Paganini

Caprice No. 24

Niccolo Paganini

Duet from "Don Giovanni"
("La ci darem la mano")

Wolfgang A. Mozart

Secondo

Duet from "Don Giovanni"
("La ci darem la mano")

Wolfgang A. Mozart

Melody in Waltz Time

Theme from String Quartet No. 2

Secondo

Alexander Borodin

Moderately; with a lilt

Melody in Waltz Time
Theme from String Quartet No. 2

Primo

Moderately; with a lilt

Alexander Borodin

Gavotte from "Classical Symphony"

Secondo

Serge Prokofieff

Gavotte from "Classical Symphony"

Primo

Serge Prokofieff

The Musical Snuffbox

Secondo

Lively, mechanical motion

Anatol Liadov

The Musical Snuffbox

Primo

Anatol Liadov

Secondo

The Harmonious Blacksmith
(Theme)

Moderately

Secondo

Georg F. Händel

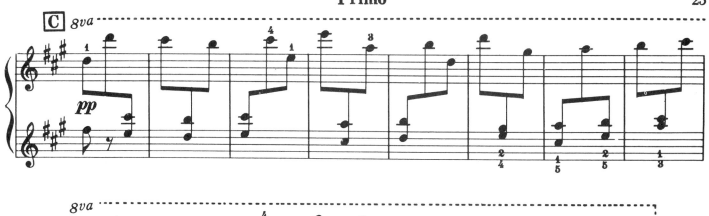

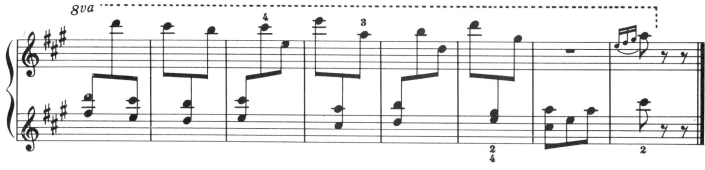

The Harmonious Blacksmith
(Theme)

Primo

Georg F. Händel

Frolic

Secondo

Béla Bartók

Frolic

Primo

Béla Bartók

Lullaby from "The Firebird"

Secondo

Igor Stravinsky

Lullaby from "The Firebird"

Igor Stravinsky

Trepak
Russian Dance from " The Nutcracker "

Secondo

Peter I. Tchaikovsky

Trepak
Russian Dance from "The Nutcracker"

Very lively   Primo   Peter I. Tchaikovsky

Minuet
from "A Little Night Music"

Secondo

Wolfgang A. Mozart

Minuet
from "A Little Night Music"

Primo

Wolfgang A. Mozart

Secondo

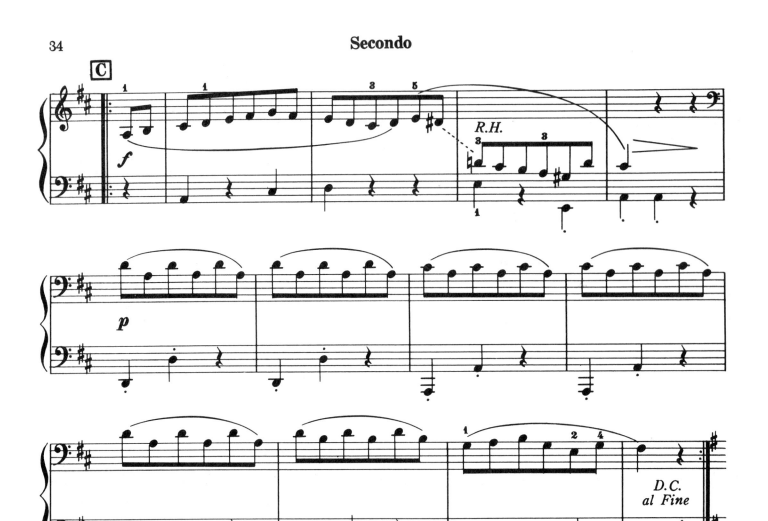

The Streets of Laredo

Secondo

Moderately

Cowboy Song

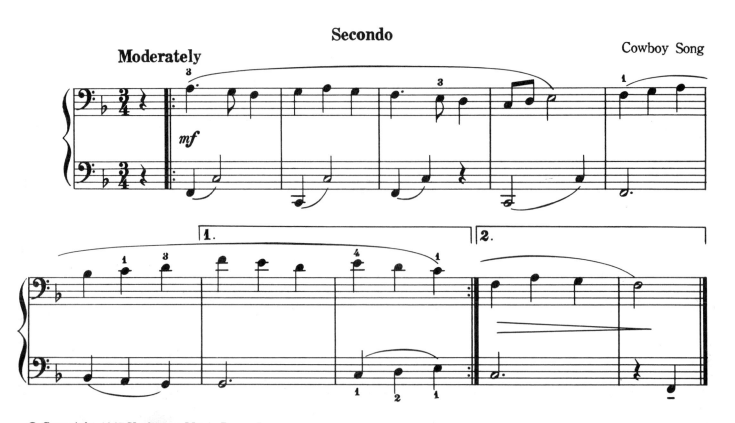

The Streets of Laredo

Primo

Cowboy Song

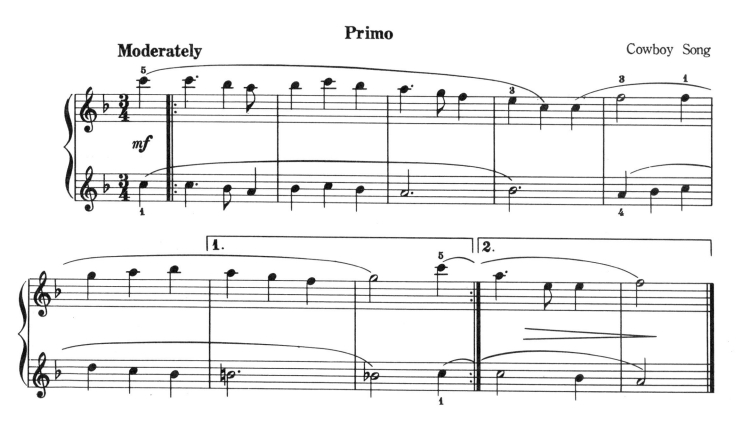

The Comedians' Galop

Secondo

Dmitri Kabalevsky

The Comedians' Galop

Primo

Very bright; with humor

Dmitri Kabalevsky

Little Rhapsody
on Hungarian themes

Denes Agay

Secondo

Little Rhapsody

on Hungarian themes

Primo

Denes Agay

Secondo

The "Merry Boys" Polka

Secondo

Franz von Suppé

16-09

The "Merry Boys" Polka

Primo

Franz von Suppé

cross over right hand

Waltzes
from "Fledermaus" and "Gypsy Baron"

Secondo

Johann Strauss

Waltzes
from "Fledermaus" and "Gypsy Baron"

Primo

Johann Strauss

Lively, with vigor

Secondo

Primo

The Washington Post

Secondo

John Philip Sousa

Lively march tempo

The Washington Post

Primo

John Philip Sousa

Lively march tempo

Secondo

Fascination

Secondo

Filippo D. Marchetti

Fascination

Primo

Filippo D. Marchetti

Can - Can
from the Operetta "La Vie Parisienne"

Jacques Offenbach

Secondo

Can - Can
from the Operetta "La Vie Parisienne"

Jacques Offenbach

Primo

Parade Of The Tin Soldiers

Secondo

Leon Jessel

Parade Of The Tin Soldiers

Primo

Leon Jessel

Graceful marching tempo

Secondo

The Banjo Rag

Secondo

Charles Drumheller

The Banjo Rag

Primo

Charles Drumheller

Careless Love

Secondo

Folk Song

Careless Love

Primo

Folk Song

Arkansas Traveler

Secondo

Fiddle Tune

Arkansas Traveler

Primo

Fiddle Tune

Hush - A - Bye
(All The Pretty Little Horses)

Secondo

Folk Lullaby

Hush - A - Bye
(All The Pretty Little Horses)

Primo

Folk Lullaby

Adios Muchachos

Secondo

Julio Sanders

Adios Muchachos

Moderate tango tempo **Primo**

Julio Sanders

Boogie For Two

Secondo

Bright; with a rhythmic drive

Gerald Martin

Boogie For Two

Primo

Gerald Martin

72

Secondo

Primo

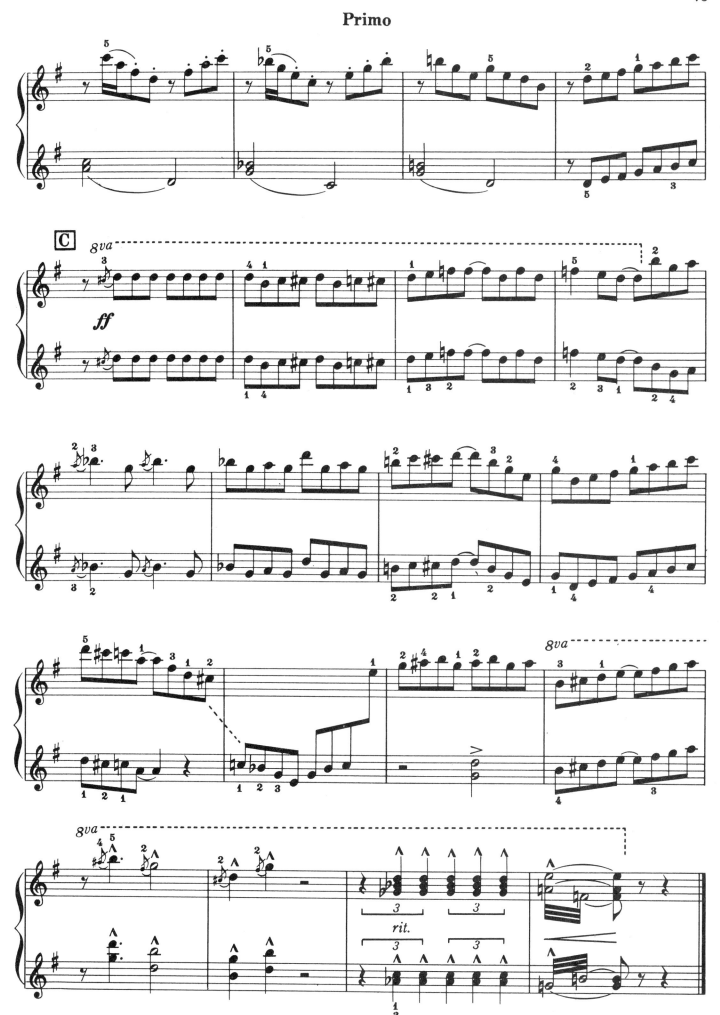

Give My Regards To Broadway

Secondo

George M. Cohan

Give My Regards To Broadway

Primo

George M. Cohan

Jamaica Farewell

Secondo

Calypso Song

Jamaica Farewell

Primo

Calypso Song

O Come All Ye Faithful

Adeste Fideles

Secondo

Old Latin Hymn

O Come All Ye Faithful

Adeste Fideles

Primo

Old Latin Hymn

Spirited walking tempo